The Repetition of Exceptional Weeks

Rajnesh Chakrapani

Fomite
Burlington, VT

ISBN-13: 978-1-953236-95-1
Library of Congress Control Number: 2022951034
Fomite
58 Peru Street
Burlington, VT 05401
01-02-2023

Praise for *The Repetition of Exceptional Week*s

This book is about family, belonging, dislocation, Anyways, a cooperative house that may not be real—What is a place?—utopia, grief, quarantine time, "routines and territories of overlapping," blurry migration, language and the body—Is genre always translation?—survival, imprints, origin stories—Can a foreigner be happy?—the intimacy of strangers, stills from a movie I've never seen. Read it and revel in wonder. The secret subject is you and me.

—Gabrielle Civil, author of the *déjà vu: black dreams & black time*

"You try to conjure layers of a place without using the words dis-place, or home, how layers of language create a loose structure of trust." "A place is a language you refuse to speak." Raj Chakrapani's *The Repetition of Exceptional Weeks* both analyzes and enacts its discourse, which is a world of careful attention to sentences that place a space, and what it might offer by way of sociality, labor, and undertaking plus all the liminal beauty that is hard to grasp. It is in this vital linking of photographs and poems that we stay astonished with Chakrapani's preternatural sentience, of what this language auspiciously affords even as it holds both ambivalence and necessity.

—Prageeta Sharma, author of *Grief Sequence*

I'm not sure which part of Rajnesh Chakrapani's *The Repetition of Exceptional Week*s is the most exceptional: the images, the exquisite language, the risk of exposing one's deepest thoughts, or the poet's heart that shows us what it means to endure in the time of contagion. They are all exceptional as they braid together into something transformative. The prose moves as image, as poetry, as prose to bear testimony to how this group survived together through stories during the COVID-19 lockdown. Indeed Chakrapani says, "These sentences on the wall are maps you can make, and the map is a translation I can share with you…" For me, these shared sentences in a quilted patchwork of intimate complexities invites us all to rethink the worn paths of connectivity, to extend ourselves, as this deft writer does, into the personal interior landscapes of those minds we think we know.

—Rajiv Mohabir, author of *Cutlish*, *Antiman* (Winner of the 2021 Restless Books Prize for New Immigrant Writing) and translator of *I Even Regret Night: Holi Songs of Demerara*

Raj Chakrapani's *The Repetition of Exceptional Weeks* is an experimental novel, a lyric poem, a book of portraiture, a plural memoir of lockdown's phenomenological rupture. To move within it is to be carried by a double current of photograph and text, like "a body of water that could be a picture or a communion," which runs with a desire for something in place of "the image and the body in conflict." Through this motion, Chakrapani locates us between the question of place and the layered and shifting map of that question whose coordinates mark what we can say of ourselves. *The Repetition of Exceptional Weeks* is a brilliant work which opens full of feeling the construction of a dislocation of being here and/or there, from here or from there, in a struggle to find our place with ourselves and among others.

— Lewis Freedman author of *I Want Something Other Than Time*

Is this you, why?
dedicated to Gomathi Chakrapani

"So my advice would be to connect with your local community or history and critically examine your own location or dislocation within the country. This will inform what, how and why you want to write."

— Don Mee Choi

The Repetition of Exceptional Weeks

2

You talk about relationships with other couples who have relationships in another place. You ask people to model for these photos and tell a story with just images. You try to write about the images but you can't complete the story, you have to come back to it with your feelings of not being from this place. Six strangers lived in a house called Anyways and did a lot more living in close quarters than everyone initially signed up for because of a global pandemic. There were rules about which bathroom to use, which floor to use, which sink to use, which desk to use, and everyone had to follow rules about cooking and cleaning during the waves of the virus while hearing about sick family members. You try to conjure layers of a place without using the words dis-place, or home, how layers of language create a loose structure of trust. A place like a familiar food, an idea of walking the center, to be welcomed and speak about money, these images shouldn't fade into the story of resilience attributed to your place.

4

Nobody can say I'm not from this place. Remember how to smell vanilla or onions, write down events to gain affection. History shows my people come from one of those relatively civilized cities. When the war starts presidents say they are glad to accept me. A place is a language you refuse to speak, how my father refuses to speak the language from his home, my mother insists on speaking with an accent, cut out language I grew up with because it's not part of the weather now. I try to tell family how I construct myself, invite them to join in some of the activities I learn in my new weather, but it's easier to let them live their life in the way they know how. Families figure things out for themselves, there's no reason to get frustrated and hang up on them. Nowadays I wear my hair long, customize my appearance, and I can't be identified to be from a place that doesn't serve my interests. Where the image and body are in conflict, I want something else. I leave a language for the complete freedom to live my own schedule, no fear that someone would find me out and put me in my place.

6

A place is where I have the wrong nose, a friend from home who looks completely different. I look up my features and the different nose has nothing to do with people and is about symmetry. I have the wrong eyes, hair color, I grow up too fast, the outline of my body writes its notes. I was born in a certain place but since nobody knows any better I construct an origin to make more sense to my knees. My eyebrows tell a different story in the place where mothers control how their daughters look with their hairstyle and too much hair on the face. Flat nose was my first nickname. I don't want to have any curves or knots on my face to be perceived to come from that place, because I am always glamorous. I want to be in front of people and I want people's attention and rewards for my beauty. You say I used to have a more attractive nose, and my hair used to be luscious, but I like my symmetry and feel comfortable telling people how I preserve my beauty which is a combination of classic features and products I use on a daily basis. I wear the most fashionable clothes even when I lose the feeling in my tongue.

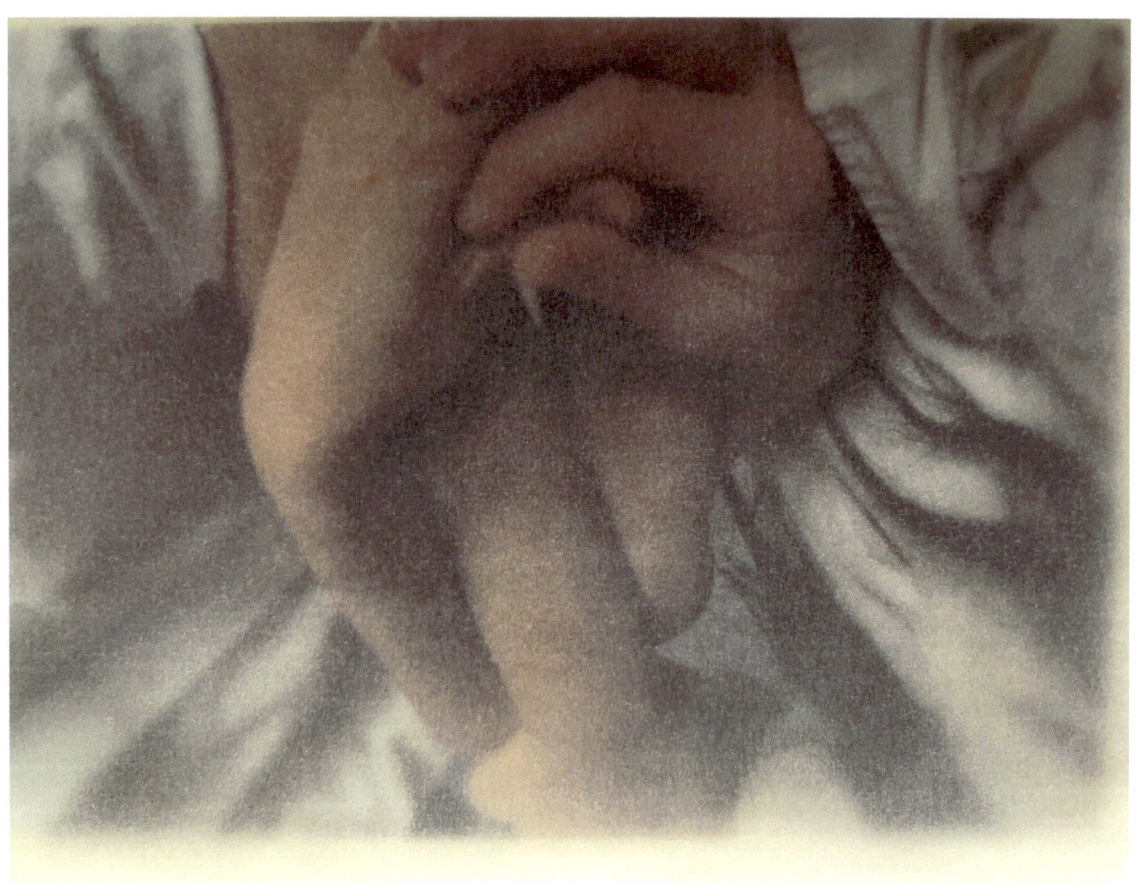

8

I don't have to worry about money, the job would be great but wouldn't change my life much. To not worry, not feel that I am constantly applying for something, whether I should commit or break up, whether I am moving forward or not. You and I never admit how the slightest setback feels ruinous. I wonder if a place can process grief, meeting people, chatting, chirpy even through illness. One person has a path forward, sacrifices the expression of emotions to give an expert position on a well rounded medical report. There is no talk of regret. A combination of military chutz-pah and new age hack your feeling, you never have a chance to say you're sad because it would turn into a task to overcome. Talks keep going on, a war escalates, a place is either somewhere you would go to fight for or stay out of the fight. I feel bad, a kind of manipulation when a place speaks that it's too tired, too old, too full of illness to pick you up and accept you back anymore. A place is healthy competition between family members, a kind of resis-tance to magic. I try to speak more about the different fantasies you and I have. Routines follow me, I don't have much to talk about, just follow me around because I'm sick and old, and I don't want to leave the house.

So you say you grew up in another place, and the other place was great. You name the people who are great to yourself. So and so is great. You measure your power in the great deeds of supportive friends. Around you people message small things about a location. A restaurant, a picture of a group of friends, a concert, a museum, come up as messages for you. You don't have emotional language to express. You try to do more, but you come to celebrations with negativity. I want to say that I'm not going to try as hard as so and so, there is a limit to stressing about having something and not having it. Not much more to remember childhood than a room that holds all your things. Every time you go back you experience and see less, and for the first time a place is without a mother or a father or a sibling even a phantom one. A place is where all the women are individualistic. They're not bad moms even though they just need their own house. Dads show up even though they are disheveled.

A place is a new family member with a clean slate, a new limb you can mold. A language you learn to speak with the dead, language you learn from a place that doesn't speak that way anymore. A place is actually saying you are from some different place and you buy flowers and withdraw money and buy a gift for the holidays and feel at home in the language. It starts to snow outside, friends don't visit you in the center. I would prefer to die than feel humiliation, there is nothing wrong, there never was, I'm just dying, my body is falling apart, I'm doing it to myself and I don't have a problem. You get over the trauma in days, but it takes weeks and years to forget the trauma about the cold, the occupation, long lines, food stolen from stores. Feeling abandoned, left behind, never fully a part of your idea that unprecedented get rich schemes can work for me.

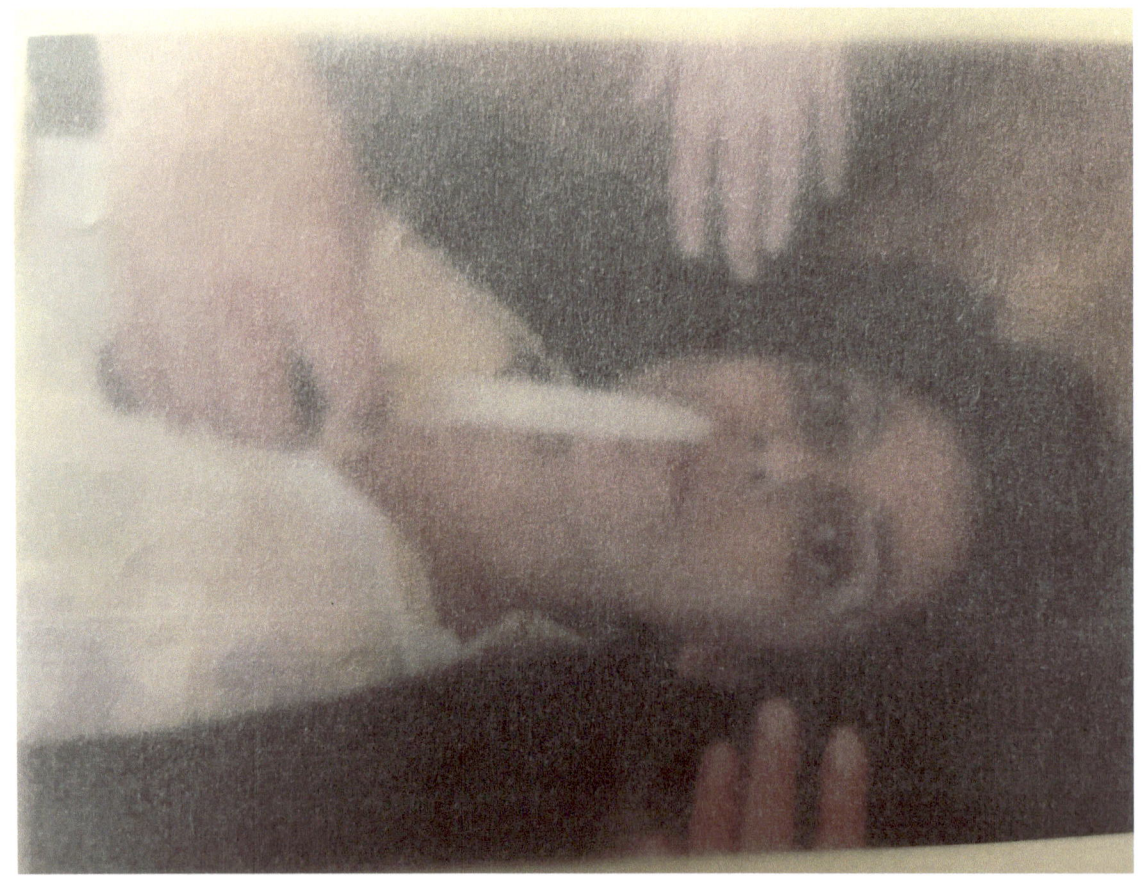

You plant walnut trees and tulips and leave food out for the cats. You keep a table and some chairs outside and a wireless speaker. It's a fine job to placate people in your family. Everything that has love around and needs protection. I organize information in a certain way, the most important thing is to find habits that make me feel confident, like a debate club. A place is when my best friend is a doctor, a lawyer is a personal friend. I date some famous personalities. You come into focus when I have to defend you. A clearly defined sense of which outsiders are friendly and I wonder if it's this staggering amount of advice that becomes a place. Advice on how to treat an illness, speculating on what the war will mean for a nation. You want more people to visit and feel at home but there's nowhere for outsiders to sleep. I could only dream of going to those famous schools and debate clubs. I train myself to read books and it's with my imagination I depart from a look. Nobody gives up power until they die, and I don't feel I have any power. So I wonder if your place is better, one complaint and the conversation stops, you have to trick someone to go to a doctor's appointment.

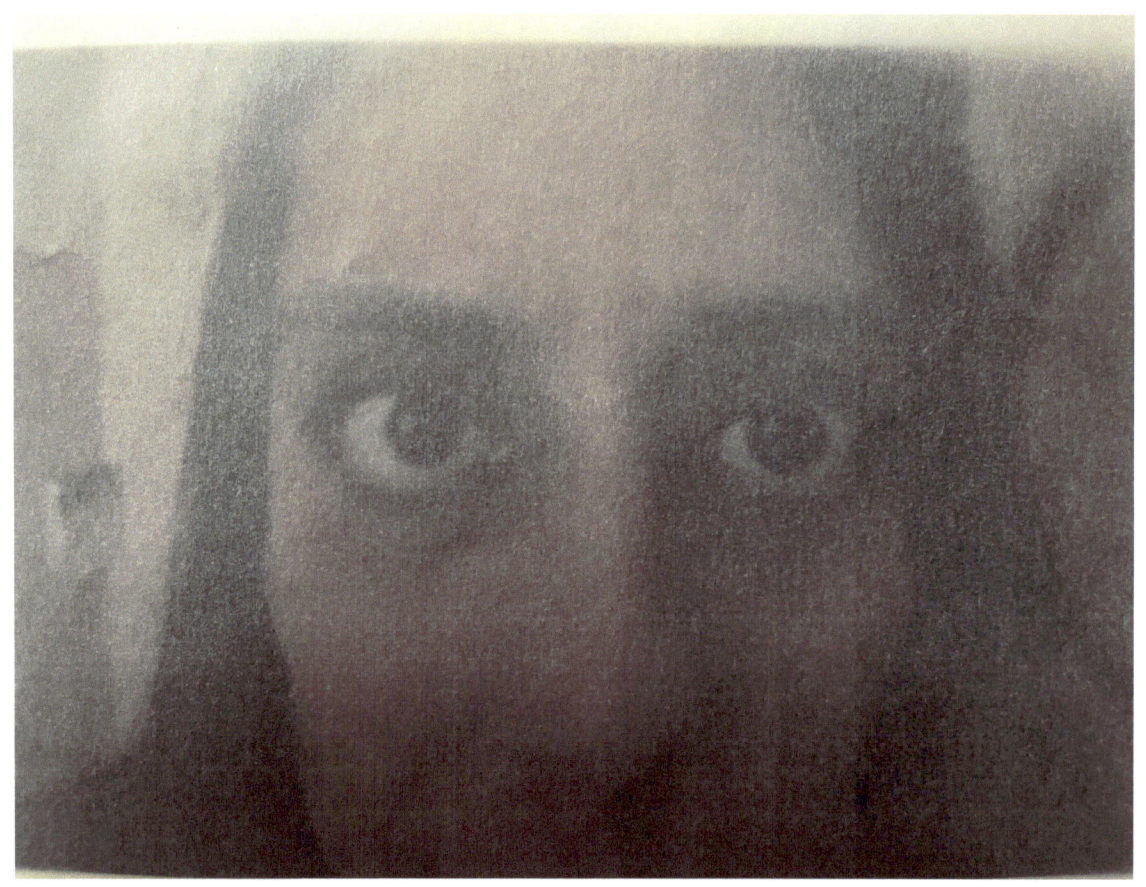

If you don't tell me something it means that you plan to take all the money and leave. A place lives with its own routines and territories of overlapping feelings and has no time for simplicity or streamlined flowcharts. I tell people that everyone is going through a lot with illness and war, they don't know what they're saying. What sounds like reason is going to be interpreted by whether my tone is gentle or aggressive, history moves with a familiar aggressive tone. Make sure a place doesn't change. The outsider gets a pass, an outsider is humored with condescending compliance.

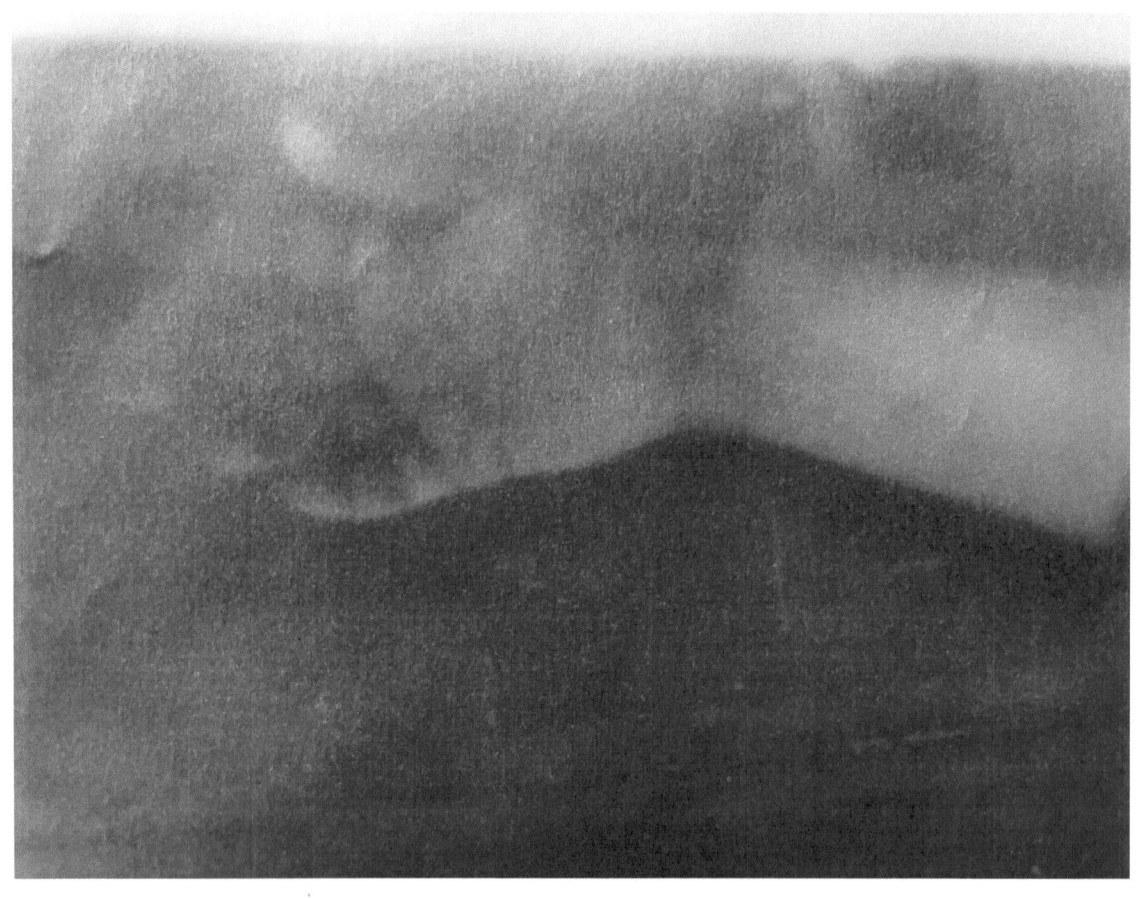

A place carries around a heroic idea of family ancestry, stunned when two people start talking again after a long time. Where a mother and daughter never fight means you need to quit while you're ahead. Dreams about meeting someone in the center, wonder why a certain place conjures a feeling of a lack of authority. A place plays the parental role, when a lawyer warns you about something and you fire up at your friends. You and I marooned at Anyways where the experience of these words was from this year or that year, and the translation amplifies a listening of the center with no date. A center imposes a rotation of building block language, or a center feels like a custodian of lingual ether.

Soft spoken people complain and get nothing done, direct language people and can-do people make roadblocks. A family knows nothing will ever be better so they speak nicely to each other. While the other place is where family is constantly in a healthy competition to improve each day. Soft and peaceful language with terror lurking at the corner and hard and tough language of results. Spend everything at once and die speaking nicely to each other. Speak kindly and there is always one more place to visit even though the hard language knows that you and I will never come here again. Language considers the fantasies of a place and talks about what will happen in the future when we buy a home because the soft syllables like the feelings of walking around the centers of a place and the warmth of the corners. Offensive language asks to do things today and the soft people leave it for a luckier time. Soft families know that institutions will always find a way to take back what they gave. Nations are not to be trusted, it is better to spend everything now because you and I have different parts in the ending. Gentle language is in the circles and roads, gentleness has a war at its borders, the news triggers memories of occupation. Soft language doesn't want any brainstorming just sympathy for the instability, floating above the stress and tensions of illness where harsh language stops talking.

Instances where something goes wrong and when I explain it to someone, they say everything looks ok. When someone starts referring to you with a Mrs. or Mr. or Sir or Ma'am, there's something off and the energy shifted. You express appreciation until a relationship dissolves because of the lack of accepting help. I'm upset that I'm not invited to all the rounds of ceremonial gift giving. A place is about whose needs need to be scheduled next. Don't talk about what's bothering you, stay polite. Existence full of financial woes, the only thing I can't put up with is a raised tone. You wonder about circles around continents, counselors who give complex advice. Where street musicians congregate, drunks gather, flower sellers make bouquets and hand them to you. Walk back in the cold with an air of entitlement to see if there are any free seats available near the warmth.

24

A place is how you complain about something, when someone keeps talking and you can never put a stop to it. I constantly interfere when I want to take you to appointments to see the doctor when someone is already doing that for you. You are more permissive and I need more structure, one side scared of sending messages and the other sends messages all day. You are not good at eye tracking items in a box, you go through a pile of clothes and can't find a pair of pants. I look and find it right away. You provide money to buy clothes. You try to talk more about the shame around money but small things make it hard. I complain the most about your tone and how there are a lot of offensive words. You look past the tone, a place is where I suck at something. Ultimately is it ok to tell someone to shut up. I wonder sometimes why I am on this earth, and put on my shoes to go out then take them off. The door always needs checking whether it is locked.

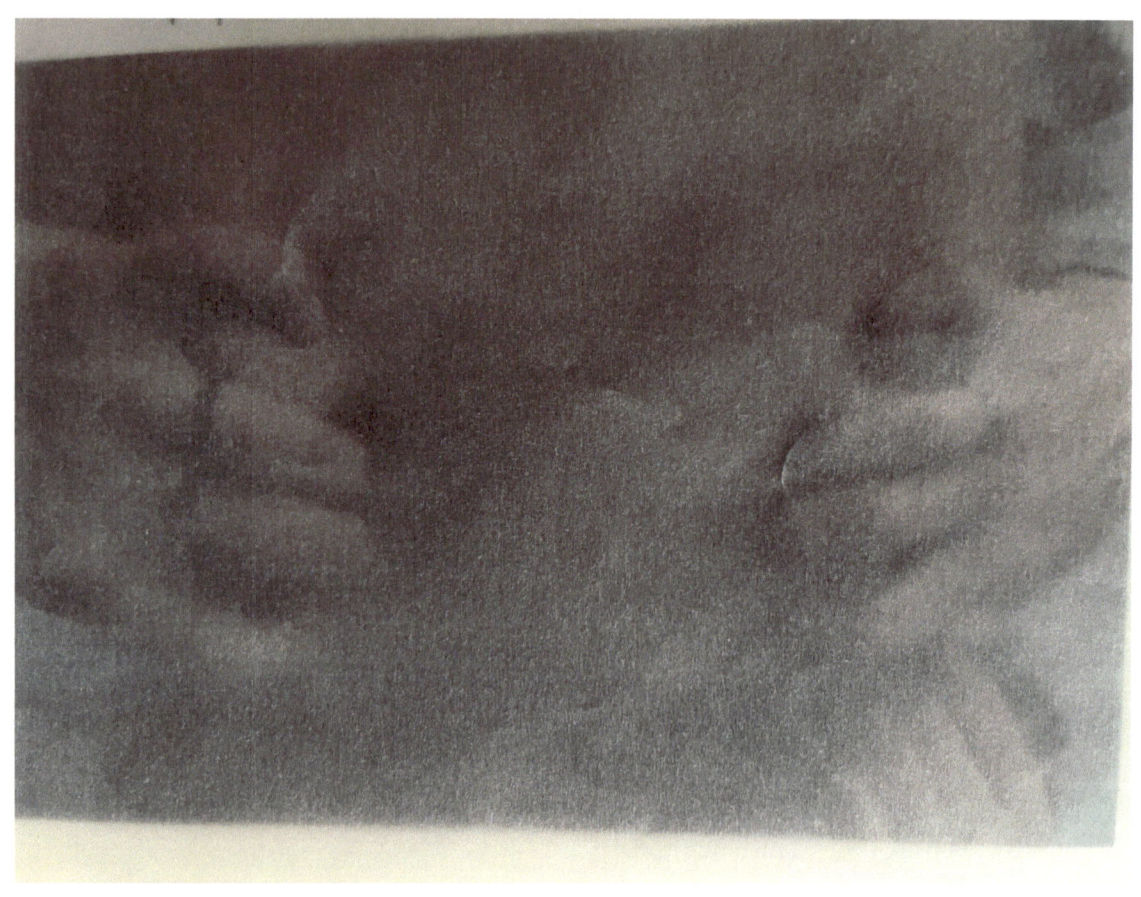

Some people start to use umbrellas outdoors even though it's February, you can't keep up with the tests, it's better to not know what's happening and you have so many forms to fill out. I order a pill box on my recommendation list to keep your pills in order and you are happy. You try to wear natural fibers because of the micro plastics and you find eco masks and use compostable straws. I can't help but keep ordering food because I move around so much it's hard to find a routine where I can cook. You change the oils you use when you cook and the oils you use on your body, the cold showers work well but you worry that you are at an age to have a heart attack. You have an endless list of friends to follow up with and what you really need is a medical friend but you can't get them to answer the phone. You worry the information you receive is not accurate and the recommendation list keeps growing.

28

A place is when you unlock horde mode, you adjust better when you have waves of enemies coming for you, your back to the wall and three directions to shoot. Communication becomes clear during a crisis, enemies start to bring you food and ask how you are feeling but you still like to play horde mode. You cultivate friends who have the same feelings of isolation and weakness. You express gratitude because that is what you were taught, and count how many times other people express gratitude to you and come up short. It's strength to use anger to express grief. Everyone wants your time, and you sink into a feeling that you have no time for yourself to buy new gadgets, try on new fitness trackers. Exercise for a few days then stop. You complain that people want you to do things consistently, but you only want to do things for a week and stop. There was a time when people would visit each other almost every week and now it is once a year. People return with a vengeance on your screen, you go back to survival mode.

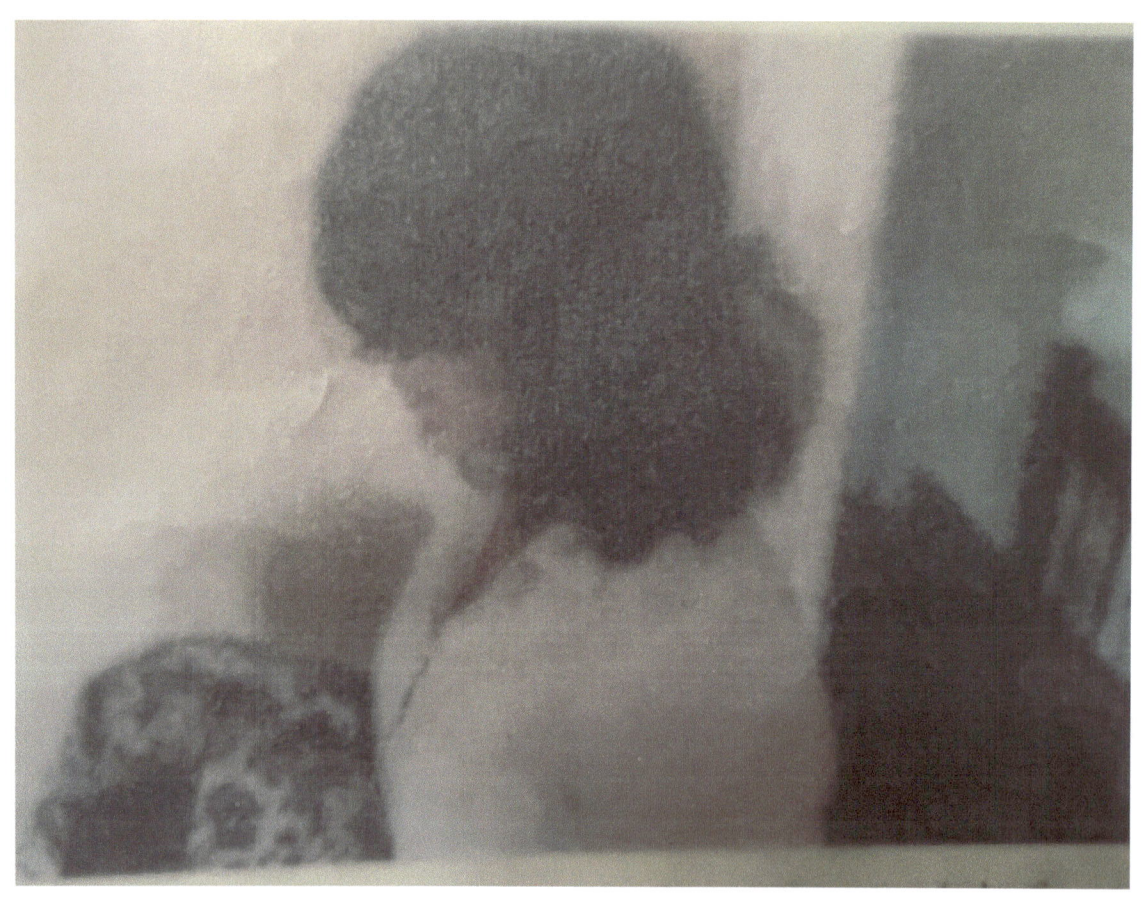

What would it mean for my body to be the center of attention? But I don't want to be the center, I don't want to engage. I shut up when I have something to say. I feel hurt, people prolong the fight, people keep going on and silence my complaints about behavior that should not exist. I don't tell anyone I'm a ghost. I'm upset and increasingly take hours of me time, distract myself with feeling I'm at the top of my game. I walk the streets of the center, most days it is warm in February. A land of firmly outlined legs. I read the street names, posters and signs, hear people talking. Remember signs I obsessed about as a child, I wore on my shirt and put around my room, now I think most signs aren't put there to speak to me. One language picks a fight with everyone and keeps in touch with no one. Sentences that close and open a center that doesn't damage me. Another language keeps in contact with people in neutral messages of no content.

A place tells a story of two people when it's a group of people feeling failure and approaching World War 3. People who can't stop the destructive addictions and try to add healthy habits, like reading a book about habits. I haven't done the first task you ask me about, you say you can do it for me but that feels like pressure. A cascade of questions and I have to somehow be involved. The list of tasks marches forward, sometimes there are explosions in the collaboration. Enjoyable plans become so intense that you look forward to the days off from them. Slowly the messages start to increase, reminders to see the doctor about your dying organs. The messages are for people ten years older than you and you wonder why you are receiving these messages at a time when you are the most doubtful. You sign up to receive notifications and ignore the messages, the important questions are buried in someone else's notes. Messages from the doctor come in the form of social media, air brushed messages. You follow the trail and reach a fitness video about rock hard bodies and families who get along so well they appear in videos with each other.

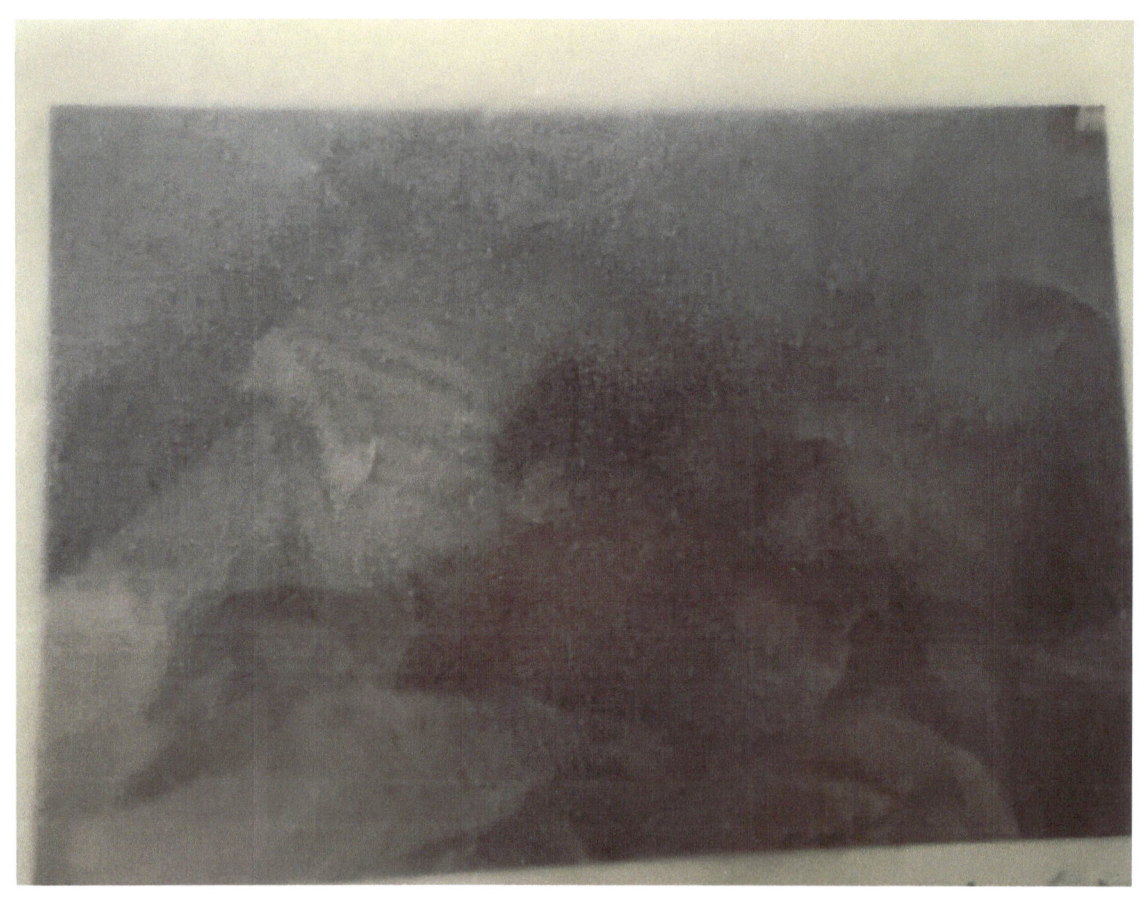

A stranger understands the language but doesn't speak it. A stranger lands the interview, and the questions make them feel bad. Today you go for the virus test, tomorrow the CT scan, you wait for the results. A stranger falls in love with someone because they have the same gestures, the same way of speaking, the same way of moving as a place in a picture. You're more concerned with what I will eat when you don't cook, when you don't do the laundry or clean the house, what will I do? Every day is a day off. Even after the stranger visits several times, they are still a stranger. You were supposed to use this time to exercise, stay thin, you were supposed to use this time to meditate, take a wellness course, start relaxing hobbies. You were going to spend time with your story. The idea of planting something comes to mind and you water other people's plants. You check how many steps you walk. You were supposed to give up some addictions, you pick up a few more, friends say it's not that bad. You spend time in bed, wear nothing, because where you come from how many clothes you wear is a sign of health. Other people's hobbies and ways of staying sane encroach on your space and you read of explosions where one country invades another. You think you have no justification to be here.

A place is promoting your language even though you don't have one, where the I comes in a costume. Family members interrupt mornings with who says harsh words and who apologizes, where you feel tired and mark "fair" on questionnaires about sleeping. Recall the ways you've supported someone else in a time of need. It's not that you don't want to see a therapist, it's the scheduling that is daunting. You wake up at 4 or 5AM and start to meditate. You only have dreams when you nap not when you sleep. First attempt, second attempt, you keep your sleep in a pile in the corner. You move the pillow around, the sheets touch the floor, the pillow falls off the bed, your feet are dirty, you shake your leg and I kick you out of the bed. I want your warmth, but you sneeze loudly.

38

How to make better ultimatums

A place to talk to someone else and find out about people through other people, talk to Grandma to find out about Grandpa and try to find out about a cousin from another cousin and about how friends are doing from their spouses. You ask a question and never get a response then ask a follow up question, ask for a confirmation and someone gets angry. Whittle down a message to a single sentence. You find out about the emergency from someone else. When there is an illness, a fatal condition, you ask for details from someone you talk to everyday, not the person who is sick. *I thought all this was self-evident.* A cousin moves to a faraway place, a brother-in-law loses their job and goes through a spell of anxiety, someone has a baby, you're not quite sure what cancer it is, an inevitability of sickness when you think and feel for a question with no practice to answer.

40

You that prods and cradles the tumor and I doesn't want to cut the toenails. I tells you to go alone and you has a big fight while the I gets off. The moment of marriage for I and the incandescence of an affair with you. You collects archives about ancestors that I can't remember, I hangs out with people while you are the artists. I searches for a place that hides and you glares with a need to return to an insufficient home. You a person that dies and I present as what is real.

42

It's easier to write about dead people because they have nothing to say. How do you write about living people without causing harm? Do you want me to experience this drive to sacrifice everything, not something I just decide? In an earlier place your uncles didn't see doctors or go for medical tests, two of them died of heart conditions in their fifties. Dental and vision concerns treated sporadically. Now you don't have to wait two weeks to see a doctor, you don't have to bribe someone to get better treatment. If you want to skip the line it's good to know some doctors who are your friends. Why get B- treatment when you can get A+ treatment? A machine is either thirty years old and still works or there are brand new machines you have to pay for and change your insurance. You want to save but there is no point because it won't cover a fraction of the medical costs. You go down to the low income insurance and think it works well until you start losing weight.

44

A pleasure to walk around the same streets, the same center and language, in circles with you. When we walk together it sometimes frustrates you when I want to lead us in a straight line, a walking so different that we don't meet just barely brush each other by. Wonder how I could afford to live in the center until I can with an uneasy feeling of usefulness. After a while a language stops talking to me. Another language wants to talk to me again after a while and pretend nothing happened. Anyways is a cooperative house, has almost no bugs, once had a mouse. It is a house of feelings, housemates design posters that say Anyways a house of language. I talk to everyone because that is my thing, set boundaries and don't mind when people bypass them, get riled up. I ask you about the medication and you tell me you can't afford the cost in this place.

You send messages and the response goes somewhere. You read the advice columns and gather up advice about people from different places, it all comes down to hearing. In the place of my childhood it was a sign you didn't make have enough money if you were thin. People would visit our home and tell me to put on more weight. Family members think children are an insurance policy, children sign a contract to care and nobody asks for something else to do. Family divided between those who regularly see doctors and those who avoid hospitals altogether. Some people don't want to find out what hurts, it could be worse. You should have six months of emergency money before you help anyone else. Hold it together, when you invite a friend the wheels go off because the friend arrives late.

48

Dads don't show any feelings occupies a certain place. I refuse to take the fall for your screw up. My wants and desires come first, not yours. You can't choose two inner circles. A series of reassurances and the rain lightly falls over a war. A reassurance not to be excluded again, after you make a decision to stop excluding. What would it mean to entirely surrender, capitulate and the other side ignores the capitulation? Fight with the transparency paper you bought for the photographs in your fist, rain on paper, creases make the images look like someone has contortions and lumps on their face. You try to hide the anger, try on the coat of a place, try to justify the purchase, you go out and buy a scarf, two bags.

50

During our call you talk for thirty minutes and at the end I say good job, you're doing great, I love you. The shock of reading a description of a place that is yours but sounds like someone's else's. A friend reminds you that you walked the streets of a romantic city looking for a brand of soap. Every morning a family member wants you to call, they call you the name you had when you were a baby. You can do nothing about the guilt. You walk around and buy clothes and food. You are in the process of not caring, buildings in your neighborhood bought by people who ignore the earthquakes.

In school you and I were taught that a place is a construct, so how do you attack it? When did you learn about a nation? Nothing in the end is made up, you attack a place because it is part of your periphery. You set up tables and run back and forth to find old packaging so you can be aligned with people who believe in your place. You tell people you will support them with money for weapons, you have family backing. You can write messages because someone will underwrite your mistakes. *Be strong for your mother.* The city is full of people who speak a different language, the different language is your language. You bump into a support group that is in a neighboring nation. You think because you are a neighbor you can just move the table. You go around and add words about joining a place.

This hallway at Anyways where the housemates made the house dog play tricks, we asked her to jump over increasingly higher rows of toilet paper. This hallway where you and I put up posters. In my dream the fridge is flooded and mom is in the other room. I'm in the kitchen and she's trying to contain the flood in the bathroom. I shout for help but she does not hear me. The city and neighborhood slowly wake up and I revisit fights I had with a cousin. Nobody says hello unless I pull on their shoulder. I do something one way and enjoy it so much it becomes a nightmare. You say you have trouble breathing unless you are in bed.

After many years you see the home where you used to live and say, *No, I don't know this place, sir.* Walk up and down streets and argue about finances. The extra money is for people from a certain background. I get hurt when you explain it to me. Because of your upbringing you don't trust anyone. When someone doesn't trust me over and over again with no evidence to the contrary that means I am a kind of person. Tough words from both sides, but I still share the money, make notes, share everything I have. You and I buy transparency paper because we wonder what people we love never told us they would like to be appreciated for. I think I can be the exception to the image of making a lot of money. You don't trust me because I make decisions without including you. I want you to say that I am a genius, you are lucky to be around me. I want you to say that I can teach you to take up more space. There is more to circling around cities and fighting. You like apartments with dusty old furniture because it reminds you of history, where it was traumatic to work in the 90's or 2000's. You bring up that I haven't talked to my brother in years.

Translation as a chance to say goodbye

You apply for a residency card. The officer reminds you of a place you forgot about where you couldn't say goodbye. He asks you where you live and tells you which streets are safe and which are not. You think about goodbyes you wish had gone better and what stopped your speech, a chance to explain usually costs something. But you have to fill out your history like a prologue where you never get to the main dish. *I want to have dinner somewhere with you in the center where everything is 20 minutes away. I* don't want to walk down certain streets and you say I'm constraining. Wistfulness in the packaging of home. Directions and recipes feel close to a language with no arms and legs.

60

Whose hands I had kissed...

Is there a scientific method to tell the story of so few people during a pandemic? A burden on those remembered to remember. I hear names blister out from other people's interviews and recollections. A whole place haunted, the way photos shimmer behind a transparency, most people die after they survive. People who protest are the wives, sisters, mothers of people left with a closet full of clothes or a handkerchief to remember the dead. After some days the tests come back and the news is not good, tumors on the liver, a large mass grows in the abdomen. The tests don't show which organ the mass is attached to. More tests, a biopsy. Then six weeks before any news, the doctors are at a conference. Feels like every day you eat a box of eclairs.

Life in the cooperative house Anyways isn't easy. You and I sleep on discarded mattresses with no proper beds. Spring we sleep on torn sheets and bedding, winter with space heaters. I wash my hair with herbs the housemates at Anyways buy in bulk. Sometimes the hot water doesn't work so I look for times when other people aren't showering. I find I can wash at night by turning the spout on and off quickly. I look for an area of the room where the sun shines so I can warm up. The sink water is freezing, every time I wash my hands I can't feel them afterwards. Through all the cold, dusty furniture, and communal cooking, I don't get sick. I get sick from where I work. At work I commute a long way and stay for long hours. Then I quit working outside. At least I have people around. And I don't hoard anything when the virus arrives.

Meanwhile the fever you have continues. Some people around you take the test and others don't. You test negative and the fever continues even after the cough goes away. You travel to a different country where 8000 protesters take over downtown. That country's lives matter and you don't want to mention the country. The lives of all the truck drivers matter who snarl the border and taunt people wearing masks. *You may be fined, you may be charged, there may be consequences.* If it were you you would be in handcuffs. In a surprising move the housemates at Anyways vote to remove various liberal policies like equal payment for groceries and allow the person who makes the least amount of money design the system.

I have never been asked to provide sperm. A land where most of the men have beards and the women are petite, an island where bye and hello are the same word. You make a joke that there's always one more island to see and you keep hearing it's better there it's better here. You try to guess what island they come from but they're not really from anywhere and are more interested in telling you where to go. A birthday, a medical appointment, a showdown with a housemate happen at the same time. Many of your loves start with someone trying to show a place to you, to describe one, to imprint childhood on you.

An island says a lot about you, the local and foreign pieces. Wherever there is an island there is a smaller island with your brother's house. The island does not allow cars. The calm streets are for barking, braying, scratching, screeching, growling. You ask about the house of the dead writer, who used to live on the other side of town. You read the dead writer's poetry, feel his teeth in the island. You continue to return to the restaurant called little road but it is always closed. I want to protect you means I want to protect myself from your feelings. All the while a lump grows on a screen in a stomach, you ask from afar about a treatment, a pandemic creates an extra quiet. Losing weight slowly over a screen, cheek bones, forehead, teeth wither away.

I swim for the first time in the Mediterranean. The temperature outside is 15C, and I see the rocks straight through. You talk about not knowing how to swim. If only I had learned something when I was young. I get angry about the amount of luggage you brought with you. I have to carry everything and in order to make myself small, I cut things from my bags. Your father. When you're alone he picks you up from the train station. When I am there, he asks us to take a taxi. Rules for luggage. No books. One exception, a book you are reading, which after you finish reading you leave behind. No souvenirs, resist the urge to buy trinkets for yourself. Don't buy gifts for other people. No shopping. Get used to wearing the same clothes. *I cannot tell you how we moved. I had rather not remember.* Accessories like coats and sex toys in transit, a kind of pantomime of intimate bodies on a budget.

One sweater, one jacket, socks can be worn for days. Outer wear is bulky. You read the dead writer's book of performances, scripts where the dead writer does not speak the language performed. You go to the dead writer's house, the guideposts are erased, someone else lives there. You move from restaurant to restaurant. The menu has items from the country they are at war with. Sometimes a country sneaks up and takes some islands. Or they take dishes from a country and change the name to sell to tourists. You make dishes from home in your own kitchen and put yourself on the menu. When the food is served, the chef, the waiters, and staff all come out to watch you eat. You try to talk to someone in the restaurant. You try to talk to people on the stone path to the beach. I tell you that the person you are talking to has a problem comprehending you. It's not the language, it's the development of the words, some-one can't even see you, you are a prepared response.

Kitesurfing is an extreme sport or dream of where to die from someone you meet at dinner

You leave the continent for the islands, where you go through the breakup. Live out your days while you watch the kitesurfers and drink coffee. The story of how people on the island gave you a chef to cook all your meals, how your friend gave you a house to stay in for free. Your friend asks if you do any W.O.R.K. Someone takes care of you like a sick grandparent, takes you on a wheel chair through the island and up the hills to the ruins. You want to go back to school but you're on an island. Everywhere you go you wonder if you are safe, there are places you feel could break out into civil war at any moment. You talk about politics during dinner at a restaurant with a couple who are on their last night before returning home. They ask you about affordable housing and you say you rent to a couple with a baby and would never raise the rent on them. Your cleaning person helps you get your passport. She is such a hard worker, you say. *Three kids, a master's degree, the nicest person.* You have your passport six months later. In one place a driver shows up with a car and drives you around for a week even though you never asked for it.

You interrupt people at dinner and make friends, the privilege to interrupt people. You talk of friends who disappear into a place kitesurfing with no wind. Build up a network of friends who are wealthy. Everyone should consider a membership at the Four Seasons that comes with free massages. You think that the place where you get your passport is better than where you came from. You embrace your father's side of the family, you tell people about the place of your mother and how they catcalled you. You cursed back at the catcallers in their language. You don't know where you will go after this, but it will be a place with no guns or bullies. On the island you finally think to yourself *I am safe*. When you call your old home, the person you used to live with has thrown out all your books and clothes.

78

See yourself as a cowboy. Fight those old wars, save the children. Protect the town, the women, with your old muskets. Worship your angels in the room. You're in your old cabin with your dog, the cabin walls have your three muskets. All the times your life is horrible and you want to throw it away. You use old muskets when you could have some new Glocks. You keep thinking *I can't believe it's my life* as you walk down the street. Your mind is the smell of the damp street. You walk down the street with those old rusty muskets. What normally happens with old rusty muskets that have been around many wars? Honor the muskets. Honor the triggers hanging on your walls. Think of your angel in the room. You don't need new guns. You don't need those new triggers. Go out to a tree and bury those muskets.

80

Anyways had a garden in the front planted by Magenta, everyone enjoyed the tomatoes, kale, and cilantro. Two of the members of Anyways begin to listen to commentaries on the Russian revolution. Gladis finger paints and canvasses for the Democratic party. A hesitancy in the way she explains her food habits. Her best friends are a group completely separate from Anyways. She comes from a time before small things begin to disappear. A time period between a war, with frequencies of friends and people to date more centered. Gladis is more successful and fastidious at holding a lockdown.

Green beans. Or how to keep writing with exceptional handwriting.

A dab of this, a pinch of that. Cut the green beans. Light processed with demolition of smells and bodies. A place where communication takes place with huddled objects, food, blankets, gadgets. Put them in a bowl and cover them. Images meant to ward off questions, a body of water that could be a picture or a communion. Microwave for five minutes. Furniture in straight lines and jagged shape memories. Roast some mustard seeds until they pop. A natural trend to reminisce about the journey reflected in the trees. Roast some urad dal. The backdoor of a chronology. Cut a chili and roast it for a minute. Not abandoned but no one lives there. Add the green beans, some salt and turmeric. Cook for five to ten minutes. Add shredded coconut. A hesitancy to turn the lens inwards. Objects next to where someone sleeps. Cook for another few minutes.

Each person who lives at Anyways has redeeming qualities. Magenta a great companion during board games. Sage's awareness of racial stereotypes enlightening. A complaint from Sage about the feeling of abundance in the house. Everyone spends too much on groceries. After some months Sage makes everyone change the system of groceries so that everyone monitors more closely the money they pay for food. Then there is the equitable payment of rent, some rooms cost more, others less. They have all the rooms remeasured, so people pay by square footage. The matter of chores, Sage is less acquiescing to slacking off, everyone must to do their weekly chores. The toilet cover needs to be down when people flush. In a moment of frustration they call the housemates *rich, white ladies*. They organize complaints based on a hierarchy of race, gender, and queerness. Housemates become enablers of systemic racism no matter who they are.

Please don't forget about your flu shot.

In order to translate I want to live happily ever after I have to ask if I lived happily ever before. What is most important is the story you tell yourself about me. Lots of arguments about putting your stories into my stories, like that dead writer said you use reality to write fiction and the fiction becomes reality. The disappointment of how you see me, not wanting to speak but the words spill out. Even when I invent a fiction you find a way into the descriptions. I hear a phrase from another language, fear of a block of salt falling on your head. I imagine pink salt crystals, a Himalayan lava lamp, words, a threat at the edge of the table. I break off a piece of something you say and flavor food, before language sits comfortably at the table next to me. At any moment a fear of what is untranslatable falls on my head. Reading is translating the word, an uncomfortable habit.

Three years ago you canceled our credit cards. Last spring you woke me up in the middle of the night, impulsively drove off and left me at Anyways. You are angry when you drive. When you have a car you are volatile and when you don't have one you erupt. You get angry when I say I'm your mouthpiece. You and I have a week of peace then two days of escalations around the idea that a place is a moment when you remember to relax and read, sit on the porch, sunbath. I find sunbathing weird. The first thing you remember is not talking. I grow up in the complete opposite way. Your house was full of educated people who thought more about appearances and had dreams of being historians or economists. At Anyways everyone sits and eats dinner together. Every time it is your turn to cook you make a big production of cooking mac & cheese, green mac & cheese, mushroom mac & cheese, difference cheese mac with brittle toppings.

You choose a new home because it has a dessert, an ocean, a mountain, the way someone talks, a mark in the language when two parts of you suddenly join. The dead writer says space and time are unimportant when you ask *If I were another on this road...* You find a way to tell the story of the truck drivers who block the road, the protesters in the capitol. You send the message to the gatekeepers of money and balance your budget. You marry the dead writer who talks about maps and translation. You withstand someone trivializing sacredness. You don't enforce the tyranny of your place on someone else.

Good morning. Happy Birthday of your favorite Ganesh. Love. Good Day.

You wear the garden, the stretch marks of the city, you wear billowy clothes. You make a place, a backdrop, a torn up background, chewed up photography, you travel some crease. A piece of thread falls out, an experience of opening and something unexpected falls out. As the years went on the feelings pushed up through the lie, new information changes the need to have the same past, history goes through intimacies. Feelings that impregnate the mind, even unwillingly, a place is the teaching of language from the mother but who does the writing? You look for the writing, the documents, try to fill in the spaces but first you have to keep deleting the credit card numbers the computer memorized. To make a new history not oppress the old history, you ask someone to tell you about a place, even one you already know.

94

Good morning. New New York news. Tornado and Subway flooded.

Translation is eating an octopus live. You arrived two hours ago. Take a cold shower. Help lower the beds. Call mom. You see patterns, to pattern something is so fundamentally you. To hunt something in a language, to remember someone as atmospherics, to come back from being hunted. Language as a disappearing act, words on a pamphlet on the disappearance. Language is setting up obstacles for an invitation, a kind of banter you make before the finish line, a power suddenly reduced. The people who know better made to feel less. What is the managerial class of language? You speak, even when you're not speaking and it is the excursions I love, when you don't legislate what is useful. Language is the commute, acting out the colors, not normally sorting yourself. First you must respectfully look at something.

96

The morning is too early for a shipwreck.

You've been talking about being of a place, a map that tells you all the places you were shy. How would you other in your own language? A map that shows how you vibrate differently in your head, torso, and legs. Can a land be a mystic place? In the news you read that you're borrowed place leaves all the translators in another country to die. Maps where translators run after vehicles. Maps populated with new words like lesbian because lots of people don't like the word. Some places are to hold hands and other places aren't. Maps where you drop in, monitor, where people can't predict attraction. It's a bit larger than your map, but you include cities that still have hospital beds, still tend fractures. Like an outer gravity, is there some way to write about place for people who don't have one? You don't just want to be pieces of a place.

I've been thinking a lot about the idea of genre that you have to hold a genre and not something in the middle. I have all these possessions to deal with. Some people talk about the story as a man giving birth, an idea of birth being parasitic and co-dependent, something other than a mother giving birth is horrific. Sight and being in proximity to a lack of agency and choice. Even if I have a choice about looking and language I choose relationships with no choice with children. Maps create a sensory route to the mind, a grid, a way of looking with plenty of lines and dots. Make it sensible. *What are things that take more time?* Failing a love in reverse. You begin to creep on me.

This what one man come and done…

The opposite of being known for just one thing. Somebody's rhythmic speech makes you uncomfortable until you hold them. The body has a leg up on bliss worship, hands as a space for thinking, all the words bumped. Objects pull together and apart repeatedly, people and their backwardness. Maps how someone speaks, how someone breaths as they go. A map is not the kind of speech that can convince you of its proper use. A map describes the looking, interrupts and obscures the look. To look when you cannot look away. Maps as a kind of hands, a thoughtlessness against authority. Hands are a way to touch your heart when you speak. The map shows that nobody is an expert, a community can be just one person. Hands play badly with each other, touch the dryness, feel warmth. Maps are a babble of noise under the talking. Perhaps a map can look at what is scattered and magnetize the hands. Touch eyes to body. Lists of images look like sites of death, a reproductive futurism, how a look can be placed.

Draw a map that begins with how you got here, says the dead writer. Draw a map that shows the connections and signals and the drinking water. *Is that a mountain?* you ask about a map of a big empty space. The dead writer starts with check-ins. Everyone says one word about how they're feeling, and people say angry, happy, sad, excited, tired. When it's your turn you say empty-headed. Frequently arrive late to meetings, you hear instructions as permission. The dead writer asks, what do you hate? People say different foods, weather, movies and when it's your turn you say, I hate people. When the dead writer asks about self-care, you say that you like to sleep in a closet with all your things around. The next check in is how often you talk to your parents and people speak of different times, different frequencies and you say, I don't talk to my parents, my parents talk at me. *I hate home, I love it here.*

You never want to be one of those people who carry heavy bags, grocery bags almost dropping to the ground. One of those women who do most of the lifting. But in those early days you find yourself pushing and being pushed. You gather supplies at the supermarket even though whole freezer sections are empty. In the morning you talk to me about who will be a dependent. A dependent goes back to their own country of citizenship. A dependent always has a backpack and many articles of luggage, a figure obscured by the transportation of home. You and I practice being each other's dependent. Someday you'll have to learn to remember all the little things I already sent you and you ask for again. Someday you'll have to learn to keep the touch in language separate.

Remember how you used to tell me I was holding cutlery wrong, that I used the wrong hand to hold a knife? You said you don't remember any of that. Remember how you used to tell me that there is no such thing as soft-boiled eggs? Remember how you used to know things more, you used to cross paths with me and ask me to jump across? Walking is a kind of reading. You always say you don't remember any of this. You don't remember telling me what to do and miss the idea behind my reminder. My memory is younger and yours is older so that later we became the same age. You're from a bigger country and I'm from a weaker place and now we're both soft. I need to teach someone about an uncomfortable place.

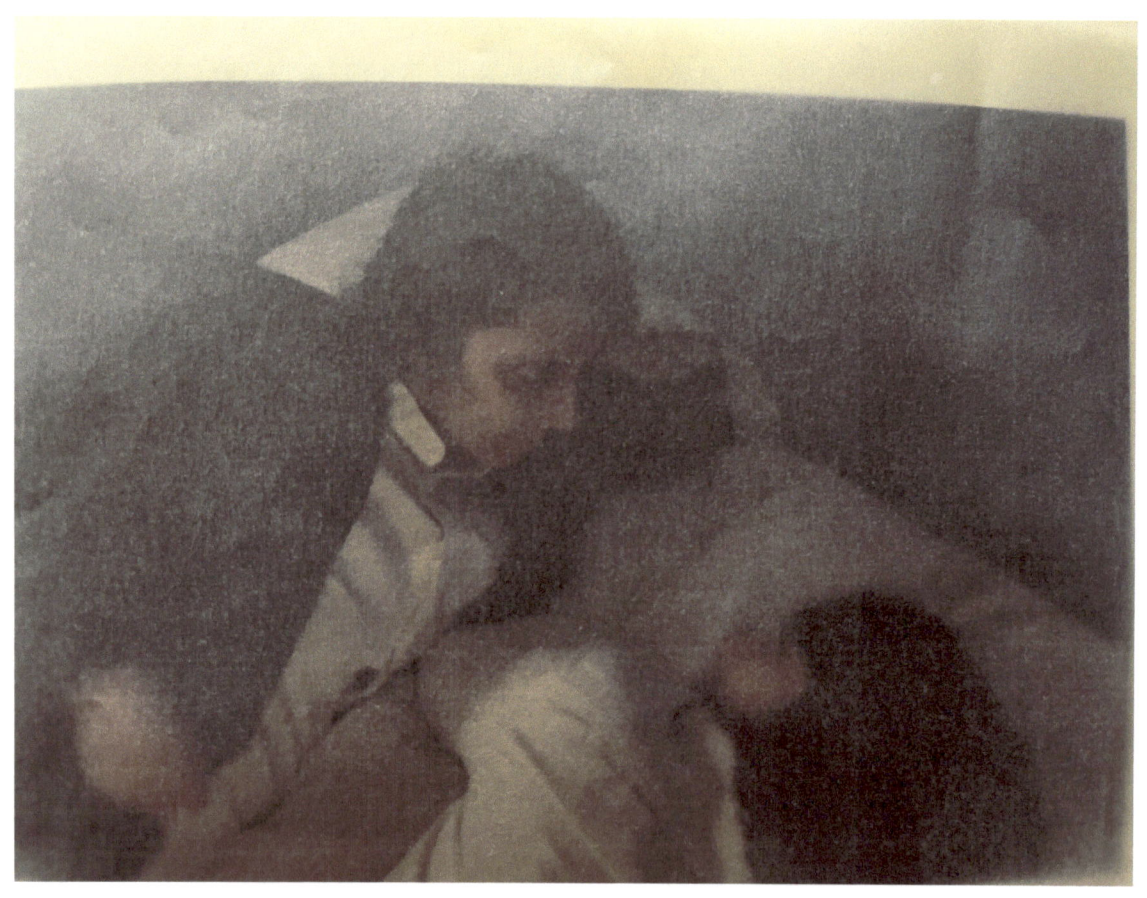

When you said information is only going in one direction did you expect a reply? You plan for a delay not the future. You preempted phone calls by saying *no talk of cheering anyone up.* In the beginning you wondered why the lights flickered on and off and electricity seemed to have a mind of its own, as if when somebody couldn't pay the rent and asked for help the response was a blackout. Each time the news says the future would resume there is a postponement. You try to move ahead in the communication but the meetings and constant need for consensus is a roadblock. *At least someone said something* is a refrain and the atmosphere is *just answer the questions* but the texts and the greetings create more chatter about coffee pots and composting. In the meanwhile, somebody relabels the kitchen drawers and spice cabinet, starts a garden, switches bank accounts, tries to adjust the thrown off inventory.

110

In the early days there was always new stuff coming. The messages at the beginning were conflicting and few people were comfortable with the idea of walking as a place. One of your first memories from Anyways was a party where everyone dressed up as if they were going to a fancy restaurant. You remember the free flow of articles of clothing, how one person supplied all the costumes for the house. You remember the instant dance parties, the impromptu musical mixtapes and the long nights roleplaying in a faraway land. You received many phone calls a day and you dreaded the calls because on the other side was a frantic sister, mother, or father who had a specific task or need you quickly forgot about. Dogs walked the people at Anyways, routines and activities made everyone sane and able to continue in the days of not going out.

You grew up with very little knowledge of the interior countries of family members, distant cities with no place, names and cities mixed up like first and last names on a pair of dice. There were no photographs, or recorded texts, with no family history all you had was a sense of creepiness, wanting to always creep on someone. In school, history is understood in multiple choice questions, no reckoning for the land that spreads in you. To name your needs is honesty but you don't name any *I*, you can't remember any living authors, you have a memory of carefully constructed rooms, tended lawns, houses with large backyards and people wearing ties and suits in photos. You accuse people of tough love. The reason you are here is because of tough choices, neighborhoods planned so nobody can drive straight through them. You live in the spiraling centers and notice that many of the houses have gardens in the front just like your house in Anyways.

Maps were hard to understand. In school you learned that more complex maps must be better. You remember where you lived for two years. Gray nights spent in a cavernous kitchen while the rest of the housemates stayed in their rooms. You spend two long winters there and one person leaves the house but nobody moves in. The friendships at Anyways are based on the floors people live on, conversations part of some underneath place. When I met you, you had come to Anyways to attend school. You were studying the history of the jukebox. Both of us had other attachments, lovers still in the picture. In the beginning you hated your classes and would stay home cooking complicated recipes. You had a started to collect recipes from home that you wanted to share with me.

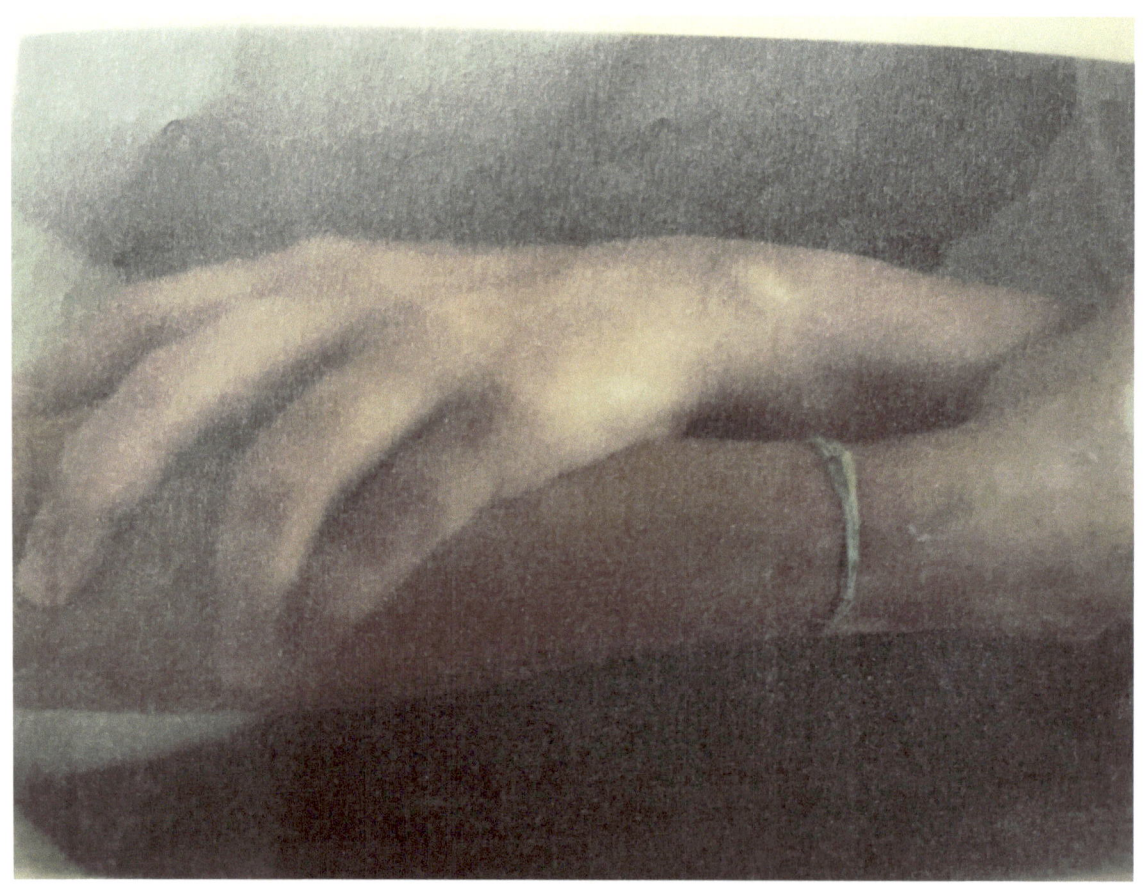

116

Like the way your father tells a story, he leaves the most import-
ant historical moments as an aside. Like the way he never throws
anything away, in his kitchen he collects dozens of thermoses and
you ask him why does he need so many and he answers *the extra
thermoses are gifts to give people.* Translation is not just between strong
languages. Words travel through jumping-off places. Look down
and see something later because you haven't learned to feel in a
certain way. Maps make your home look like other people's cities.
You feel you are in a children's story and you think with a kind of
heroism, make homeland in places that try to destroy homeland.
Something opening in a failure to fill in the gap. A map with mark-
ings shot through with holes. The maps might be torn but that's
where the feelings are hidden. Before you began to translate you
learned of the dead writer who predicted how things are going to
happen.

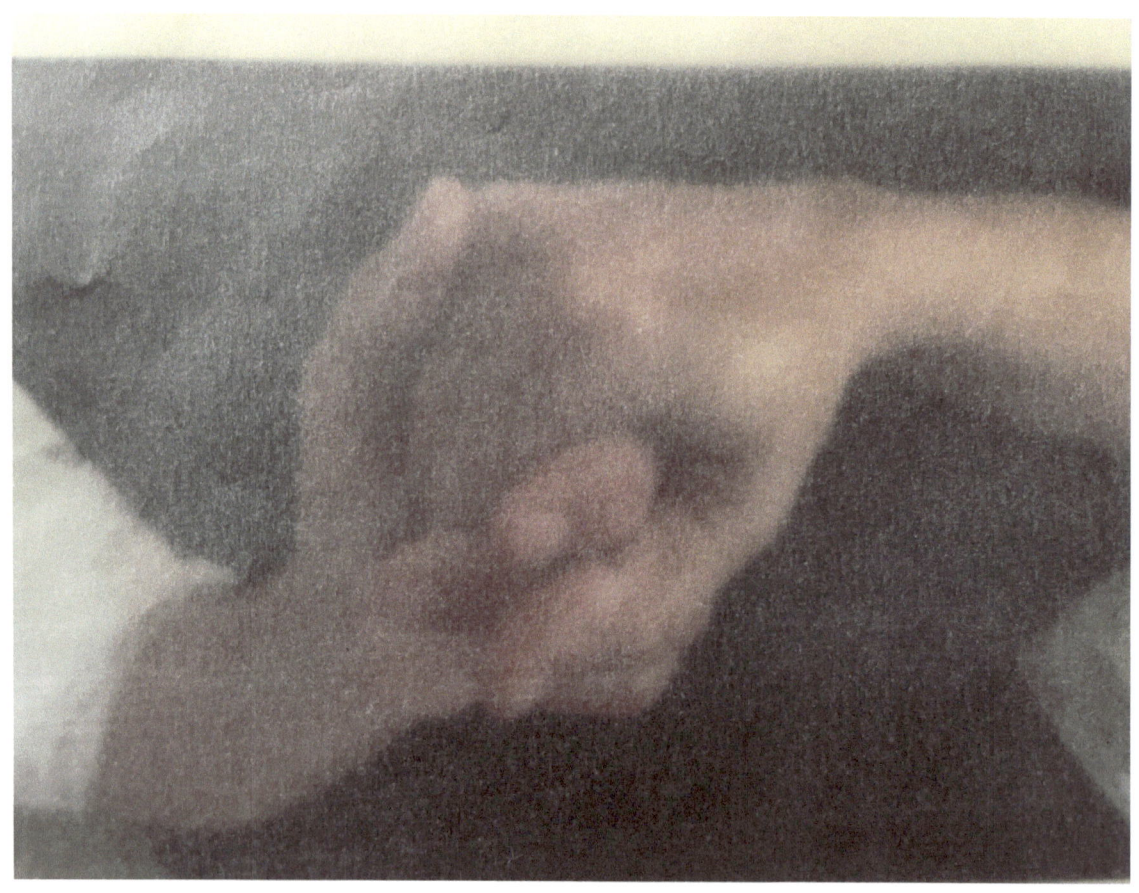

If you refuse the first gaze and make a map as a scientific proposition, if everything has a name and a value like a botanical garden. The drill makes a hole in the wall and a hole in your diploma. The map points to where wealth is accumulated, the drill is the sound of labor through the monologue and every time the story starts it is interrupted by the women who screw. Translation is a form of care, a way of dealing with fear. The care comes from the wastelands of the city, from people not born in a language who take ownership of a language. *You will not be able to find the sky in a locked room* is a translation. The beauty you feel from pictures is a fantasy required to fuel you. These maps are a testimony that time in literature is relative. It's a lot of labor to keep memories and you have to learn your own body weight, serve multiples of yourself, ideas better off with no grammar.

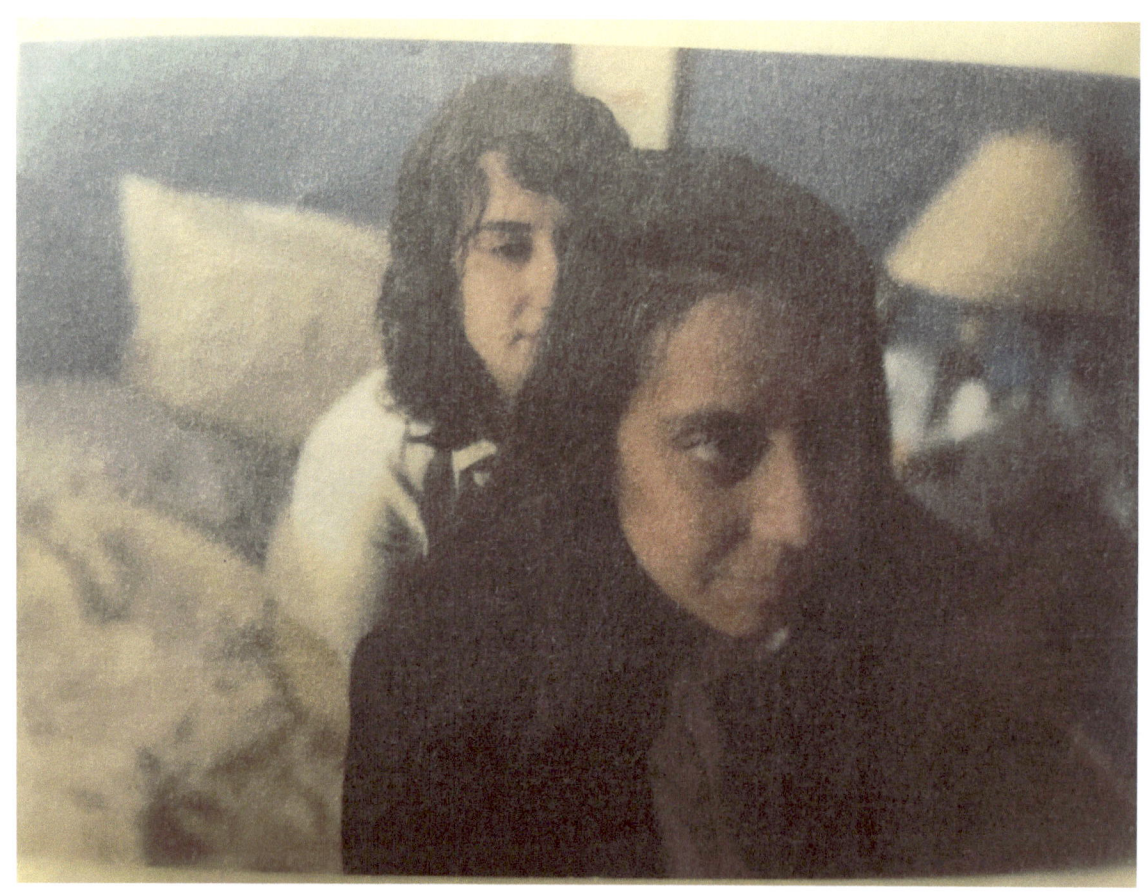

These sentences on the wall are maps you can make, and the map is a translation I can share with you, even though you already know that people jump on rooftops to walk through a city. Maps from school books used to show home as a territory from an above gaze. Maps that drew lines which you later drew in dots. Maps that drew holes in walls, a cartography that pretends to be complete. Camouflage is a message from all sides, neighbors who tell you your home is beautiful, the walls are your own. Is a place taking sides? Always the presence of a dead writer in your translation. The English says it's not about you, it's always a becoming you.

Acknowledgments

I'm grateful to The Margins and Bennington Review for publishing early drafts of these poems.

To Mihai Moroiu from the Fulbright Romania program for his encouragement of this book.

I made the images in collaboration with Paola Messina, Anjali Jaiman, Nikki Dodd, and ATM (dog) for which I am thankful for their trust.

To Prageeta Sharma, Sawako Nakayasu, Gabrielle Civil, Madhu Kaza, Rajiv Mohabir, and Elizabeth Willis who in real and imagined ways inspire me.

To Lewis Freedman, for his generous reading and feedback of an early version of this book.

Some of the poems came out of my participation in an exhibit on Palestinian Translation in Berlin 2022. I feel in debt to my fellow collaborators Sondos Zaghari and Christin Alhalabi. To Andrea Cassatella, Max Weiss, Laura Menchaca Ruiz, Nadine Fattaleh, Ziad Faraj, Hmidat Omar, Jens Haendeler, and everyone who participated and attended the exhibit.

To Ioanida Costache, Jessica Kashiwabara, Carlo Dure II, Sitha Sithalakshmi, Sachin Mehta, Samprajani Rout, Nikhil Narayan, Shirish Balachandra, Shobha Mahadev for their support and friendship during the time of writing this book.

Some thoughts for the images came from the International Center for Studies into Communism, Women Enemies of the People, an exhibit I viewed in Bucharest, Romania 2022.

To the Iowa Writers' Workshop for time and community to write.

To my parents, who provide a space for me to create even now.

To Ramesh Chakrapani, for holding space for my memory performance.

And to Anca Roncea, just to spend a day with you in words means the world.

Index of Poems

Fomite

Writing a review on social media sites for readers will help the progress of independent publishing. To submit a review, go to the book page on any of the sites and follow the links for reviews. Books from independent presses rely on reader-to-reader communications.

For more information or to order any of our books, visit:
https://www.fomitepress.com/our-books.html

More poetry from Fomite...

Anna Blackmer — Hexagrams
L. Brown — Loopholes
Sue D. Burton — Little Steel
Christine Butterworth-McDermott — Evelyn As
David Cavanagh— Cycling in Plato's Cave
James Connolly — Picking Up the Bodies
Greg Delanty — Loosestrife
Mason Drukman — Drawing on Life
J. C. Ellefson — Foreign Tales of Exemplum and Woe
Anna Faktorovich — Improvisational Arguments
Barry Goldensohn — Snake in the Spine, Wolf in the Heart
Barry Goldensohn — The Hundred Yard Dash Man
Barry Goldensohn — The Listener Aspires to the Condition of Music
Barry Goldensohn — Visitors Entrance
R. L. Green — When You Remember Deir Yassin
KJ Hannah Greenberg — Beast There—Don't That
Gail Holst-Warhaft — Lucky Country
Judith Kerman — Definitions
Joseph Lamport — Enlightenment
Raymond Luczak — A Babble of Objects
Kate Magill — Roadworthy Creature, Roadworthy Craft
Tony Magistrale — Entanglements
Gary Mesick — General Discharge
Giorigio Mobili — Sunken Boulevards
Andreas Nolte — Mascha: The Poems of Mascha Kaléko
Sherry Olson — Four-Way Stop
Brett Ortler — Lessons of the Dead

Fomite

David Polk — Drinking the River
Janice Miller Potter — Meanwell
Janice Miller Potter — Thoreau's Umbrella
Philip Ramp — Arrivals and Departures
Philip Ramp — The Melancholy of a Life as the Joy of Living It Slowly Chills
Joseph D. Reich — A Case Study of Werewolves
Joseph D. Reich — Connecting the Dots to Shangrila
Joseph D. Reich — The Derivation of Cowboys and Indians
Joseph D. Reich — The Hole That Runs Through Utopia
Joseph D. Reich — The Housing Market
Kenneth Rosen and Richard Wilson — Gomorrah
Fred Rosenblum — Playing Chicken with an Iron Horse
Fred Rosenblum — Tramping Solo
Fred Rosenblum — Vietnumb
David Schein — My Murder and Other Local News
Harold Schweizer — Miriam's Book
Scott T. Starbuck — Carbonfish Blues
Scott T. Starbuck — Hawk on Wire
Scott T. Starbuck — Industrial Oz
Seth Steinzor — Among the Lost
Seth Steinzor — Once Was Lost
Seth Steinzor — To Join the Lost
Susan Thomas — In the Sadness Museum
Susan Thomas — Silent Acts of Public Indiscretion
Susan Thomas — The Empty Notebook Interrogates Itself
Sharon Webster — Everyone Lives Here
Tony Whedon — The Tres Riches Heures
Tony Whedon — The Falkland Quartet
Claire Zoghb — Dispatches from Everest

www.ingramcontent.com/pod-product-compliance
Lightning Source LLC
Chambersburg PA
CBHW041616120626
46551CB00003B/460